MORT'S
Country Store
AND MORE

by Patricia West

illustrations by Steve Sanford

Harcourt Brace & Company

Orlando Atlanta Austin Boston San Francisco Chicago Dallas New York Toronto London

Mort York liked used things
that were worn and torn. So he
opened Mort's Country Store.

Baseball
cards 5¢

Mort's store was full of worn and torn things—sports cards, storks, forks, short cords, horns, corks.

One morning, a woman came to the store. "Your corks and storks are worn and torn," she snorted with scorn.

But another woman said, "I like all sorts of worn and torn things, Mort!"

"Why do you like worn and torn things?" Mort asked.

"Come to the porch at the fort in Torch Park in the morning," she said. "You'll see, Mort!"

While doing some boring chores, Mort thought about the woman some more.

Mort thought more and more
while he snored and snored.

In the morning, Mort went to the porch at the old fort in Torch Park.

Mort saw paintings of a port,
a thorn tree, four horses, and
a shore.

Then he saw the woman.
She had turned his worn and
torn things into art!